dear warrior

A POETRY COLLECTION

WRITTEN AND ILLUSTRATED BY

georgia stavs

dear warrior

dear warrior,

life brings us battles; loss, heartbreak, betrayal, rainy days. things that make us draw our sword, that pierce through our armour. pain that rocks our very core, that shatters us to pieces. that make us question why we exist to face the tragedies that make us human. the aftermath of survival is an eternal fight to heal, to rise above each wave that crashes down on us just enough to inhale a sweet breath after much too long underwater. to feel sun on our skin, to feel hope again.

our soul, the energy that animates our flesh and bones, seeks to experience. to navigate as many lessons as possible. it is ferocious, child-like and curious, magical as flowers that bloom in perfect symmetry through spring and the ocean current's perfect timing. mystical as the moon moving tides and the sun shining to give all living things their life. we are pulled from the same parts, crafted from the same materials; *you are a miracle.*

life is our soul's journey, a series of challenges and how we deal with them. how we heal from them. how we look at them, and how we learn from them. dear warrior, this collection of words was written to remind you that you are never alone in the darkness, and there is always a sunrise on its way to the horizon. to reveal to you the tiny spark within you, the magic that unites you with all things living and the universe itself. that sets you divinely apart in all the ways the world needs, that can rise from spark to lantern to torch to phoenix as you feed it.

to remember the magic that you are, the ancient wisdom within, and the fire burning so brightly inside you even in your hardest moments.

I

the darkness

dear warrior,

how do we begin to understand light? without it, to our eyes there is nothing until we feel around for a match and ignite. before man put spark into glass attached to a switch we fumbled around through the darkness. we lit fires and gathered, told stories, sang songs. we basked in the glow of moonlight and admired the stars knowing the sunrise was never too far off.

it is easy to feel the sun on your face on the bright days, to say "I want this forever" forgetting growth requires darkness and rain. when we are planted and the sun feels far away, we crave the return of its heat. we crave our peace back and weep. it is hard to remember that both dark and light serve their purpose. we forget that the pain we endure creates the character we use to change the world.

though a flower is beautiful in bloom, each petal must eventually wilt. the plant goes on. it will spread its roots deeper into the soil to drink up what it needs, grow new leaves to soak in more light. and when the time is right and the growing is done, the flowers will bloom with bright petals once again.

the seed will always burst through, the morning will always burst in and proclaim that the darkness does not last forever. though winter's wind feels long and endless, spring always arrives to shake the earth back to life.

it is difficult in the shadows, where the roads are treacherous and unknown; it is trauma and open wounds and struggling to continue on. these rains can wash us clean and prepare us for a new beginning. these tears will water the roots for us to grow.

until then, you are not alone.

to you,
with the weary spirit
and tired heart,
to the one fighting battles each day
with a smile on your face
despite the wars beneath the surface of your skin
inside your brain.

to you,
who holds things together
when the moon cracks the sky wide open
and darkness swallows you whole,

when parts of you shatter
and you are forced to put the pieces back together
hands bloodied,
heart sore.

- hands bloodied, heart sore

I wear the night sky on my sleeves
and shove stars into my pockets,

praying they'll give me the light I need
to make it through this darkness.

- night sky

I'm caught somewhere between
crashing wave

and ocean breeze.

calmness fills me,
eyes flooded by saltwater
in a heartbeat.

how can they understand,
when they can't see inside my head?
when they don't spend these days as me?

I'm just an island,
crashed and battered
in the middle of the sea.

- island

hiding devils,
masking pain in small talk,
small smiles. bracelets,
long sleeves and loud laughter.

in laboured breath
and awkward silence.

in a wince,
avoidant eyes,
"I'm fine,"
a downwards glance.

- devils

as the dust settles,
I peel myself from my mattress.
each bone beneath my skin aches.

I tell myself,
"you can do this,
it's just one more day".

no one will know the river of tears
that streaked my face.
the whimpers turned to bellows,
battle of wills between angel and devil,
sobs I swallow down,
pain I don't let out.

I shake out the sheets,
crack open a window
and let the cold air rush in ...

tonight the angels won;
I chose to stay.
I can do just one more day.

- day by day

let me rise taller
from these fires
that torch me,
that threaten to burn me
back into the ground.

- fires

anxiety is a beast with many faces.

some days,
a tiny nagging voice
in the back of my brain
echoing softly the things I should change.

others,
a deafening scream
heard only by me
that brings tears to my eyes
and me to my knees,
balled up and rocking.

anxiety is a battle nobody can see
of the demons in my ear
trying to strangle
the spark
out of me.

- anxiety

I keep reaching for a past me
knowing she can't help me.

as I try to piece myself together
so did she;
I guess we'll just both grin
and bear it.

- grin and bear it

they say the axe loses track of the past,
but the tree never forgets
how she splintered and cracked.

I wanted to be stronger, stand up taller
but I was stuck inside my mind,
small cuts send me spiraling back.

I learned to be kind through harshness.
I learned what it was to brave a storm,
so forgive me for sometimes getting it wrong.

I mean to be tough as bark and tree trunk
to shout a victory song,
but sometimes it's only a whisper,
or a "timber"
and fall.

be kind.

you may forget just how long your words echo
in the dark spaces of someone's mind.

- the tree remembers

if you see the sun,
could you tell him where to find me?

I've been searching for his rays
in every place,
stumbling through the dark blindly.

he's all I'm thinking about lately.
I've been quite cloudy,
things feel hazy...

please,
just tell him where I am
if you see him again.

- if you see the sun

I want to build a pair of wings
to take me far from this place.

I want to catch the wind beneath me,
let it take me wherever it fancies.

I want to capture it all for a lifetime;
people small as crumbs in grids
of skyscraper, field, and skyline.

I dream of my great escape wondering
where the breeze would take me,
but I realize soon enough no distance
could be enough to be free.

no matter how far my wings can carry,

I cannot escape myself.

- wings

butterflies,
not the sweet kind,
float up from my stomach.
fluttering,
flapping against my ribcage
'til it cracks,
gently dripping acid.
this nervousness
burns.

- butterflies

some ticks
pass by
in the blink of an eye
while you're consumed with love,
happy, feeling divine.

when tragedy
strikes
as it does for us all,
each second
like hours;
chest wide open,
by each tick
mauled.

when you start to feel alone,
trapped inside your bubble,
remember,
no one's time
ticks by
without struggle.

- when she strikes

all these thoughts and feelings
surround me,
engulfing.
all at once I'm warmth,
love and rage.

flavours so familiar
with a sickening sweet scent,
enticing me to stay a while.
here I go
twirling in the spiral.

I want out,
but don't know how;

I guess I'll just steep
a little longer.

- like tea leaves

I hold the whole sky above me;
clouds, sun and moon.
it threatens to snap my spine in two.
I pray for rain to lighten my load;
to finally make me feel brand new.

- brand new

a piano's song
is incomplete
without the black keys

but god
does this pain
pluck at each of my heartstrings.

it feels
like this organ
is feverish
and deteriorating.

- these keys breaking me

shadows greet me at my door
like an old friend
who I thought I'd outgrown.

I fight against the blackness
filling the spaces around me
as they welcome themselves
and we sit down
for a drink.

- shadows

my soul silently weaves dreams of places unseen.

in the dark it is hard, but I fill in the grey
with rainbow-filled images
of a beautiful place.

where I have been
is not where I am now,
and now is not all there will be;
I can think ahead to my future instead,
float away from my bed,
see what real dreams are waiting for me.

- my dream world in the dark

I wish these clouds away each day,
as if focusing on them
will make them pass any faster,
as if the ups and downs
haven't been worth it,
as if my life has been
anything short of a beautiful disaster.

- beautiful disaster

this fog may feel familiar;
sadness swept under the old rug,
saltwater seeping from tired eyes.

you may be well acquainted
with stormy days,
know every cloud
and droplet by name,
drudging through mud
day after day.

your eyes may have adjusted
to the darkness,
lost sight of the stars
somewhere along the way ...
felt like maybe you just belong in this wicked, twisted place.

please remember
not to make a home in numbness,
not to wrap your bones
with fear, longing, sadness.

no matter the journey ahead,
you are greater than these weights.
the light that burns inside you
can cut the night sky into day.

it is safe to let go of this pain.

- it is not your safe place

dry your eyes,
tired soul;

I know it hurts, but take my hand
this isn't where you're meant to land.

- take my hand

II

lost at midnight

dear warrior,

attraction surrounds us, love calls us home. its force is the reason we come to exist, why bees and butterflies flock to flowers. why we stick down to this planet, why we want for anything and traverse the unknown. love is the space we hold in our heart that touches us deep down to our bones.

in this life we must love fiercely, as if it is the only thing we know, and yet we must also learn the ways of letting go. we may find ourselves lost, spiralling downwards in disappointment. we lose what we love dearly, what we cling onto for dear life. friends turn to strangers, new faces and places to be. love turned sour, new moments replacing old, fading memories.

the spaces between change can be unsettling and life has no pause button. this existence asks of us a great effort to shed what no longer serves us, and to move boldly towards what we love. to let go of the things that have run their course no matter the mark they leave on our soul. to hold things tucked in between ribs and in the shelves of our heart without guiding our everyday.

we must learn to let go with pain and grace. we must face the unknown with no map and a heart full of bravery.

let us meet in the in-between.

I love like wildfire untamed.

I love like wildflowers
painting entire fields with colour.

I love like the entire world is on fire;
I know no other way.

- wildfire

I dance among
glimmer and shadow,
hoping to make sense
of all these feelings,
all this shining,
these losses,
all this sorrow.

- glimmer and shadow

I've connected so many dots,
tied strings to things that I love;
people, home,
places I have
and haven't yet roamed.

threads intertwining
across the universe;
perhaps it is why I feel
constantly pulled on,
tangled,
like scattered pieces of a whole

- fragmented

I know I must shed
these old layers of me
to get to where I need to be,

but here
I still find myself
clinging
   desperately.

- clinging

I played you on a sunday afternoon,
a familiar tune,
and bopped my head along.

but forgive me,
I can't know which words to sing
when you're always changing your song.

if I bend too far for you,
I will surely break;
whistling your tune
was my biggest mistake.

- a familiar tune

you carved hearts into my skin,
drove love into me;
I thought it was a beautiful thing,
but now I'm just bleeding.

- bleeding

a spider does not spin her web for fun;
she spins to eat.

you spin your pretty stories
and have a feast of me.

- feast

bearing the shadows of your soul,
finding routine,
learning each other
outside, inside, in between.

rose-coloured blind
to every red flag,
letting your heart carry you
when your mind should see.

putting down roots,
intertwining with one another
where the soil is poisonous,
the foundation is crumbling.

nights with few answers
and fewer hours of sleep.
conversations that eat away your self-esteem,
leave you wondering
how you can be too much
and yet always
too little
at the same time –

losing your mind.

losing yourself in false hope,
bending backwards,
passing time.

- first love

I was never the best dancer,
but I took to your rhythm,
drawn in like a moth to flame.

I twirled and dizzied as your steps got quicker,
your fire roaring, engulfing me,
and I could no longer move
to the beat.

- the beat

I thought we could be evergreen,
but we were deciduous, choking down leaves.

when did you decide
you're always right?

that you could decide a path for me?

who died
and made you ruler of all things?

- evergreen

I gave you the key to my heart
but you shoved it in, slammed doors,
left tracks with dragging feet,
and tore the place apart.

now I know,
above all else,
I must guard my home.

- on guard

we all have wounds –
in this, there is no shame.

we all have days
when they are reopened,
old scars
turned to throbbing pain.

- you are worthy wounded

there weren't enough bandages
on earth to get me through;
I couldn't survive
trying to hold onto
all the sharp, jagged pieces
of you.

- you

you cannot drill ink into my skin.

my blood will boil,
heat me 'til the thick black
seeps from these pores.

you will not touch me, hurt me,
become part of me.
I will not let hostility
taint my story,
no matter how lost I seem
you will not stunt my growth,
you will not make your mark on me.

I will not let you take my hope.
I will not let you impose on me your beliefs.

these patterns on my skin will have no trace
of your negativity.

I will leave no remnants,
not a single droplet.

- ink

I longed for a hand to hold,
lips to kiss my cheek.

a thumb to brush tears away,
a half to make a whole out of me.

little did I know,
I'm as whole as whole can be.

there's no one else I needed more than my own self;
I have always been the saviour of my dreams.

- I'm saving me

don't let your mind pretend,
fool itself into thinking
it knows how things will end.

- you're no fortune teller

we scream and we weep,
as it crumbles.

as what we once knew

f
a
l
l
s

apart.

- we forget it's a new start

I keep finding myself
tangled in the in between
of who I am
and who I'm becoming.

threads of the past cross
and coil around me.

who am I really
supposed to be?

- the in between

growth is not always
e n l a r g i n g ,
it must so often be rest,
recharging,
determining direction,
gratitude, appreciation,
settling roots into dirt.

then going forward
sprouting leaves,
blooming anew.

- growth

your soul bends like a sunflower
to those who feel like light.
stick to those who feel like sunshine,
to who attracts you,
and leave the rest behind.

- sunflower

you deserve love that lasts through a downpour,
even as dreams crumble around you,
your dance turns to lost footing,
when your tears are hard to see through.

you deserve love that lights up your dark corners,
that clears the dust out,
grows flowers in the most
unhospitable parts of your soul.

you deserve a love that brings you peace,
with lull of nostalgic memories,
with a future
you can't help but daydream.

- true love

the people who love you
will not forget your value.

they will not leave you hanging
and put doubts in your mind
about your place inside their life.

they will know each tiny detail,
dog-earing your pages.
all the thoughts inside your mind,
the way you love and all your phases.

you do not ask for too much;
you just beg the wrong ones.

- you are valuable

we hold onto toxic
in fear it's the best we'll ever get,
thinking the past
is where our happiness lies.

we break our own hearts
clinging onto our shorelines.

a boat may seem safe
docked in place,
but it's meant for so much more.

happiness may be resting
just beyond your horizon.

d
  i
    v
      e

in,
cast your sail,
take the plunge.
see what awaits you
once you carry on.

- cast your sail

without wilt,
from what
could beginnings grow?

- endings are beginnings

the hell
of this journey,
has brought me

to the cliff sides,
to the precipice,
to the doorsteps,
to the mountain tops
I needed to see.

foggy paths
and dark nights traversed.
all the trails of crumbs
I was meant to find

leading to who,
where,
I was meant to be.

- breadcrumbs

the masterpiece
does not reveal itself
from the start.
it's the effort,
the journey,
that guides the art.

be gentle with yourself
as the clay sculpts.

hold on,
as you break free,
as your heart breaks,
as you change shape.

let your heart be softened,
let your mind be moulded
as you shape your vision.

- taking shape

when life turns to earthquake,
and your foundation shakes –
dear warrior, hold faith.

you can make it through every change,
every heartbreak,
every challenge,
every single dark day.

- earthquake

III

day break

dear warrior,

no feeling lasts forever. no cycle is permanent. no matter how dark and long the night seems, the sun is always on its way to break day.

each time you stood strong, like a tree through a storm, through the breaking of your heart, has guided you to this very moment. each scar you bear is a reminder of the strength you've shown in the fight against pain that threatened to consume you.

our minds become filled with doubts and anxieties. we find it hard to believe that life can be any different than the hard times we've seen. we forget just how powerful we really are, how our attention is what fills our world with infinite darkness or a sky full of stars. you are a consciousness on a human contract, meant to seek the light each and every day you're alive, from the tiny flicker of a candle to roaring blaze on the most beautiful days.

if we can let go, if we let the light pour in, this life allows us to learn, explore, be adventurous. to find beauty and gratefulness. to make all of the choices that microscopically transform us.

dear warrior, never lose hope in the miracle that is being alive for this short time on a tiny rock rotating in an endless sky. no matter the grief, brokenness, or heartache you face, your soul was made strong enough to carry on another day. pain will not forever stay the same. hold out until the light begins to break through the clouds and you can finally see its rays.

like the sun, you will rise in your full glory once again.

it is a battle, but dear warrior, *you were made for this.*

beautiful stardust soul,

I pray you find the light that has been with you all along.

- inner light

you can catch me at my worst hour
crumpled in a corner.

you can trap me between
who I am and who I wish to be.

you can talk down to me,
convince me I am nothing.
you can try to break my spirit, steal my dreams.

I am no stranger to fighting.

but know when you step towards me
with malice
you must meet me at your best;
no matter the bending I must endure,

I will not break.

I will be ready for a battle.

- I *will fight for me*

I fall,
and my god,
do I shatter;

but from these
cracked bones,
I will blossom.

- broken, budding, blossom

she is a dreamcatcher,
feathers dancing in a light breeze
while her beads sparkle in sunlight.

she is delicately crafted, weaved with care,
and as night falls, she is the one who dares
to beckon to it, draw it in.

she looks darkness in its face
as midnight strikes,
no matter how scared,
and spins it into a daydream.

she leaves behind
only the loveliest things.

- dreamcatcher

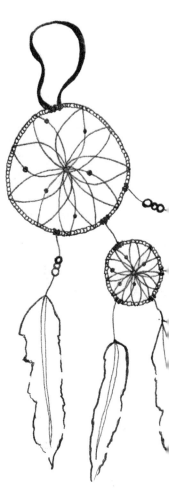

give thought to those that came before you,
a tree stretched over lifetimes
to allow you to be alive.

your parents are perhaps as far as you've uncovered,
met great grandparents,
come from blood of a royal colour.
you may have visited where you originate,
or for centuries you've rooted in the same place.

your ancestors fought
earth, wind, water and fire,
even each other,
for you to exist.
they went to war and survived,
fought for justice, better lives,
endured sickness and weathered challenge with courage.

they watched as the world changed around them,
and yet they carried on
living, loving, losing,
finding strength each day.

creating an infinity that has ended in you,
or maybe you've continued to grow your tree, too.

in you is ancient knowledge and wisdom,
the strength of this line in your spine,
carrying on until the end of time.

- ancestors

it's through untangling life's chaos
that the soul unravels its magic;
a woven masterpiece, a tapestry
of triumphant,
heart wrenching,
extraordinary tales.

- a tapestry of tales

I seek to carve space for feeling,
to find the place of calm
and steady
from which rooting can take place.

for love to grow,
for letting go,
for flowers to bloom
from the ruins of what no longer lives here.

- carving space

let the light shine into each
chip, crack and scrape
until it burns;

seal them with gold.

- kintsugi

don't worry about the shadows in your past,
keep your face forward.

remember that it takes dirt to grow.

stand tall and hold your head high.

seek the sunshine,
find the light.

- advice from a sunflower

she taught herself to fly with broken wings,

so no,
she may not glide through the air effortlessly.
she will soar
then dip down low,
hesitate,
dodge at the last moment.

you may watch her with a heart skipping beats,
but she'll prove your doubt wrong every time.

still, with broken wings, she flies.

she is a force to be reckoned with,
not the epitome of grace and perfection
but grit and dedication.

seeking sun,
scorched like Icarus,
she is not one to be trifled with –

she knows she can be broken,
yet still prevail.

- imperfect wings still fly

size on a tag
measurement on a scale
followers
tax bracket
dollar amount in a bank account
grade point average
friends
lovers
a diagnosis
an age
calories eaten
bullet points on resumes
struggles
triggers
past mistakes

- *things you are not*

smiles
laughter
times you've persevered
things you've made
dreams
kindness
goals you've achieved
love given
love gotten

- things you are

the universe did not create you
with calcium in your bones,
oxygen in your lungs,
and stardust in your veins
for you to hate the vessel
that lets you experience it all.

- your body is a miracle

as if the obsidian black
of the night sky
wasn't enough
they dropped her into a
black hole
buried;

little did they know
she's a flower that blooms
in the darkest of rooms,
the most desolate of places.

- she still blooms

there is a fire inside you,
and if they can't feel it
let them freeze.

- you are not born to please

when your scarred parts
reveal themselves
in second guesses,
insecure glances,
painful moments,
and bubbling emotions,
please remember;
your humanness
deserves kindness.

- you are worthy

things will happen
that will shatter the inside of you;

like a tower, you will crumble.

these moments will change you,
mould you and shape you.
if you're not careful,
they can break you.

you cannot be who you were
before your world turned upside down,
before your life caved in on itself.

but you can always gather the pieces
and start again.

- *the tower*

healing requires
pulling out parts
into the light,
pouring alcohol
in the wounds
until it burns.

ripping through shadows
like pieces of a puzzle
removing the bits
that no longer fit,
haphazardly shoved in.

these heavy
stories I carry.

- rewriting

strip down your title,
the dollars in your account,
the car you drive, your home,
jewelry, hairstyles, cell phone.

strip down to your desires,
the things that set your heart ablaze,
that make you feel your inner fire.

strip down past your clothes,
through your skin to your bones
to your soul and what lives there,
the things that make you care.

the things that give you a slice of hope
in cruel times,
in an ever-changing life.

- beneath skin and bones

surviving / wildfire / unworthy / chaos / too much

survivor / sweet as a peach / growing / lover / leader / the lion

- names I have known for myself

she does not just get her wings,
once her egg splits open, no –
she eats up her whole home
'til she can eat no more
and wraps herself up tightly.

no part of her remains the same
as she goes through each stage –
they doubt her,
but she knows she was born for this.

and when she cracks chrysalis wide open,
blood coursing through her wet wings,
she finally flies away
tasting freedom for the first time –
how tough and beautiful it is
to be a butterfly.

- to be a butterfly

you cannot cage
a courageous heart
or wild soul.
it cannot be captured,
bought or sold.
it will not be held back,
told what to do.
bend to the will of other souls
that pass through.

their journey is their own,
as they chase after their dreams
they pave their own way.

- wild soul

she swiftly glides,
stomach to earth,
tongue forked in two.
no words leave her lips
but she reveals the truth;
her serpentine soul
is the universe
as are we.

destruction
and transformation
are one in the same.

in cycles we spin,
her old skin she'll shed.
tail attached to mouth,
it is her nature
to heal, to change,
to begin again.

- serpentine

when good, joyful,
are too far removed.
too difficult to muster,
too many miles away.

when love is much too strong a word
for your view on you,
or on a separate page completely.

find the grey.
choose to remain
in the middle.
restore balance.
stay neutral.

- black, white, grey

that you choose to fight
and seek brighter days
instead of collapsing into the pain
is something
to celebrate.

- carrying on

your beauty is not
what lies on the outside
despite the magic of your growth;

stretching and healing,
flux and flowing,
marked on your skin.

each curve and fold,
every ridge and valley,
telling a story.

you have grown and changed;
do not punish your body and mind
for not remaining the same.
for showing the world
where you have bent
to never break all the way.

your beauty is not
just hair, skin, or smile;
it is in your story
beneath them all.

- between the lines

each scar is a symbol
of how you fought the beast

and *won.*

- *stories*

no matter what comes,
I'll clutch
my handful of stars.

- this light will carry me far

Georgia Stavs is a Greek Canadian author and artist from Toronto, Canada. Her creations are inspired by life, the universe, travel, nature, feeling, and healing. Her mission is to spread light after a life living in the shadows of anxiety and depression.

She began sharing her work on social media and writing her first book in 2019. In her debut poetry collection "dear warrior", Georgia paints through poems and illustration a story of courage, healing, and hope inspired by her own experiences. A soul's journey through mental illness, struggle, love, and finding yourself through the unknown, flowing from sunset to sunrise.